Regarding
My
Mother

Regarding my Mother

Poems

Martin Tilling

Grosvenor House
Publishing Limited

The right of Martin Tilling to be identified as the author of this
work has been asserted in accordance with Section 78
of the Copyright, Designs and Patents Act 1988

The book cover photograph is copyright to Shaun Wilkinson
The book cover is copyright to Martin Tilling

This book is published by
Grosvenor House Publishing Ltd
Link House
140 The Broadway, Tolworth, Surrey, KT6 7HT.
www.grosvenorhousepublishing.co.uk

A CIP record for this book
is available from the British Library

ISBN 978-1-80381-315-8

To my father and mother, Harold and Sheila Tilling,
and my brother David Tilling.

Thanks for the love and support of David Watt, the rock in my life

Also, thanks to all of my incredibly important extended
family of friends

POEMS

PART III

(A special tribute to Rodgers and Hammerstein's Carousel which inspired so many of the poems in this book)

PART I

ONE HAND, ONE HEART

Make of our hands, one hand,
Make of our hearts, one heart,
Make of our vows, one last vow:
Only death will part us now.

MARIA
Make of our lives, one life
Day after day, one life

BOTH
Now it begins,
now we start,
One hand, one heart,
Even death won't part us now.

Make of our lives, one life,
Day after day, one life
Now it begins, now we start
One hand, one heart
Even death won't part us now.

(Influenced by and most of the words taken from the song One Hand, One Heart, from West Side Story, the song is by Ansel Elgort and Rachel Zegler)

OUR CAROUSEL'S FALSE FIRST WALTZ

(This incident that drove this poem never happened. It is my fantasy of my mother's and my first walk to a carousel, to ride it and dance to it. Like what happened in the beginning of Carousel)

Walking alone,
Or were we led together?
We hear the rhythm's three beats,
Ringing out repeated pulses,
Spiralling our minds into following that sound

No arms together,
No partnered steps,
Just solely magnetised,
We are pulled towards that whirlpool,
And reaching its vortex we grippingly watch

As it's colours and charms enticed,
The streets we unconsciously danced down,
Showed their shining path's
enlightening of the carousel's turning circle,
And it's glamour,
And it's glimmer of a yearned for glory

That we knew nothing of,
Save our shared childlike chastity,
And our innocent desired scent of this rhythm's taste
and it's obvious existence's eternity?

MY OTHER CAROUSEL

One day, mid-nothing,
Mother announced we would start a new class,
Brother and me, now stopped in our tracks, out on our back lawn's
    green grass,
Stumbling, slowly we pulled ourselves back to the house along a
    thread-like string

Seven or eight, I cannot recall my age,
We were told we would don our feet in glossy, tapping black shoes,
Once weekly evenings, we would gather together learning new moves,
But all my body could do was stop in a freezing gaze

Gradually though, I warmed to those twenties' rhythms,
David too, I think, began to relish and yearn this un-yearned thing
    called dance,
No parental couples, just you and the music and your feet and their
    trance,
First connected time without any Mums

This tap dance, ballroom, childhood glory,
Was to give me an even greater revelation of what my life could bring,
That year, our class was drawn into the town's musical ring,
Us, on stage, them watching, a classic story

Our jaws ajar, excitement filled with uncertainty,
What would our part be? What was a musical?
This 'Carousel', we, then, could not learn, by rewinding and watching,
    it was just a blank wall,
But my young soul was soon to be enriched, almost heavenly

Father's factory hall, we are delivered to, one spring morn,
Long wait, we are told, before we will get to learn our part,
Eyes weary, soon to be staring, startled at a young girl's rapturous start,

Shoes pointed not tapped, her 'ballet' choreographed such a storm
I knew not of course then, of dance and its profound, utter
    expressive art,
But when she stood still, sighing, exhausted, after rehearsing that
    twenty-minute masterpiece,
All I could do was also stand still, cheering inside, silent, daring to
    dream that that could be me, please,
Could my life possibly be as rich and full, oh boy when could I start

Our call came, this family place's role for us revealed,
Mrs Snow, not Carousel's daughter, was to be our premier role,
Just one short parade, the showy Snow children, tall to short, around
    the stage we would stroll,
Two minutes, one day him, one day me, that's all our steps would yield

Yes, our foot-stepping was way less than that dancer's brief serenade,
But in my now spinning mind, there was no planted shortage of
    expressive yearning,
This Carousel's carousel had set my now aspiring mind's clock a-ticking,
All my life, at no time, would I ever let my artistic desire be just a
    charade

JOYFULNESS AND JEALOUSY

(In the voice of my grandmother, the joyfulness refers to my grandmother and all of her family including my mother. The jealousy is of all of the others who could not relish and easily succeed, in cooking, like her)

I'll make a real big clam-bake,
So, sisters and brothers and friends and school kid's,
and sons and daughters,
all come to feast on this warm June day,
My chest is pumping,
My arms are thumping,
My mind is rejoicing,
Whilst hers, I see, is slumping

We'll carry your pots and pans, logs and coals,
I know you all will burn in pleasure,
as you build the fires to deliver my delicious gifted treasure

But what will your role be in any future gatherings?
Fearing your anxious second-rate delivery, you will always ponder in
      your fathoming

Come search my pantries dear ones,
My puddings all sweetly, spicily, richly, moulded,
Are long caressed with ales and liquors,
And the fruit of our country lanes is picked and pickled or turned into
      delicious jams,
Over here, these crystal-iced cakes,
surrounded inside by soft yellow binding,
which keeps this fruity celebratory offering always ready for sharing
      with all

At school, my white kitchen hat, remained floating above my mind,
As I delved into those kid's huge hearts,
Filling them with plentiful dishes to help keep them willingly entwined,
And you, and her, and him, my little ones,
Relished, cherished but also blemished with your blushing cheeks,
Rush to share your mother,
And her love and her offerings to all

Fittin' for an angel,
Fittin' for an angel,
Fittin' for an angel's fall

JUNE IS BUSTIN' OUT ALL OVER

(In the voice of my mother)

The summer that made me happy,
The day I met my man

I danced a jolly dance
in my mind and in my room,
As I agreed, to join my sister, or a friend,
For that years Friday ballroom calling,
to her village, my village, maybe his village

A dash by bus, to Banbury Cross,
A sweaty, attempted, cooling stroll,
Down that town's street to its regal hall,
And now, here we are, twisting and whistling,
Tossing our coins in hope of a partner,
Who might catch the dance's rhythm,
and glance at our eyes, in longing temptation

Two soldiers or sailors, stepped around the dance room's door, into
    that halo,
Coloured in blue, sealed in uniform tightness, they shone out to all on
    that longest day's night,
Only one was leant the line of my path,
Taller than his mate, his gait drove his seeking body forward,
Hand held out, lips smiling, in surprised ascent,
He burnt his touch deep into my soul,
As upward we together stepped, reaching out to the bustin' June
    sun's moonshine

WHAT'S THE USE OF WONDRIN',
IF HE'S GOOD OR IF HE'S BAD

(About me thinking about my mother)

Just because you love him and he's your son,
That love should have been enough,
What's the use of dreaming, if he's like you, or if he's not,
He's your son and is from you, he is not you,
So, touch and dance, in a joyful connected trance,
Not a trance of worrying steps,
Nor a touch for tainting his love,
Nor a dance, where arms and rhythm are not in line

So, I try to delve into her mind, and her wondrin',
Long before her eyes looked out for him and me,
Youngest child of sweetest folk,
Delicate soul, demanding of caresses,
Grew up to be for whom?
She sought, but knew naught,
Stitching her thoughts through her daily chores,
Knitting her wishes and filling her evenings long,
Connecting a tied knot to another knot, in her school's worthless
    learning

When I remember her weakness,
I cherish, reflecting her goodness,
Hands, with which that seamstress was eased,
Hands, whose finger's flustered over a pen's words,
Hands, toyed to properly cut the meat of truth,
Hands, harmed by too many untold falls,
But hands, which held her head up, as she smothered those she
    chose, with un-divided faithful embraces

Hands, those certain, not those uncertain, questioning human hearts,
Never wondering or measuring the goodness or the badness,
Just touching and feeling as it was,
They can only let go, when love's pulse ceases to fuel the warmth
    of their gentle lifetime's hold

THERE'S NOTHING SO BAD FOR A WOMAN THAN A MAN WHO THINKS HE'S GOOD

(Reflecting on my mother's thoughts of my father and me, and thinking of the Carousel song with this title)

I've never understood the words of this song,
Why is it bad to be good, if, you feel that, to you, only they could belong,
But then, how could you know before, however much you ponder long,
I guess that's the point,
No knowing who will disappoint?

But a man who doubts himself,
Would end up putting himself on the shelf,
Maybe not, if, as a sailor, he gets in his uniform dressed,
Or if the other one just knows how she wants her boy to impress,
Both uncertain youths they were,
But shine they surely did to her

Transfixed we were, caught for ever in her loving embrace,
Our transmitted goodness, tangled in her selected place,
Never, we thought to turn to bad,
That, would eternally leave us truly sad,
What is it, that a woman can clearly perceive as wrong?
No-one knows least of all her chosen two men throng,
There's nothing so hard for a man, who's hooked to a woman who
    says he's bad

IF I LOVE YOU (OR NOT)

(From the second verse, this is in the voice of my mother)

She sings, he, in the background, waits,
Yearning, but knowing her learning,
Would charge her coming passions and fill her time with questioning
  lessons

How would I know?
What would that mean?
What would you know?
How would I know what you meant?
But oh, if I loved you, that wonder I would dream

Your hand would be woven into my heart,
Your touch would delicately tingle each time we reached,
Your hair would be matted, stitch-like with mine,
Creating the glorious tapestry of our future together

But then, I might sit, sadly miserable, sometime, knowing I had lost
  your love,
Or that I never could see its clarity,
How might that mistaken mis-step maroon my soul

But no, this my love could not be wrong,
I shall give and never choose to lose what I gave,
Nor shall my well-rounded sight find what should not be found,
What is formed between two kinds, will stay,
My touch will never wander afar from its most gentle caress

You, that certain man, closest to my heart,
Will walk and rest besides, never will we part,
And those that come from us, will always be with us,
I know that that too will be...

TWELVE AUNTS, FEISTY ALL

(About my grandmother's large family)

Of twins and only being twins, they must have known naught,
We often counted their so many names, and always lost track of our
    consciousness,
So many sisters and their two brothers,
In that small house so close to where our house was to be,
Their half-timbered Bishops Tachbrook home, full of those running,
    spellbound kids,
How must that have been?

Who would go to the water pump?
Who would go to the chicken farm?
Who would go to the bluebell wood?
Who would go to the station pub?
All those days you were service girls, to landed folk,
Oh, to have met you then, would have dissolved me in such joy

All sure and certain, strong and loud
Save Grace, the youngest and longest to live
Opposite my choirboy home, her welcoming place,
Where she, Grace and her man, Perce, lived so well
Audrey, Doll and wait, their brother Son,
Who else?
The others were the most feisty ones, or at least these three had
    always said,
Con was the other and the only name that resides,
But all twelve feisty lasses now lie besides,
Touching, pointing, growling,
but smiling and embracing as their souls rest each alongside

13

MY SISTER BRENDA "SNOW"

(About my mother's sister, the picture on the inside front cover is of them and their brother)

Big one she always was,
But not bigger, just bolder, than their older bragger he,
Brother to them, son to her, cousin to cherish, and worshipped they
    all knew he was,
Hands holding firmly their deepest bonds

How did she, the most well one, live so childishly?
When daily they both seemed destined to diminishment,
He coughing and breathing, long and tough, too toughly rough,
to surely catch enough breath to breathe another breath?
She angled small, reached upward longingly,
Only to be taken almost rhythmically, suddenly, down by too sharp
    angles,
Just staying afloat as the ship shook her out of that moment's presence,
To find herself sadly still alive, scared and scammed by her precious
    life's wishes,
And now so clearly feeling her thirdly titled order,
And all her small world's madness at her always mocked "sick" sickness

She lived long enough to be sure of her worth,
Not their measure of that,
Just her strong clarity that to maintain her value,
She would need to act,
To them, to mother, to all those who would come,
And then, unknown as it was at first, to choose her certain man,
Upright and first to be found and left with great cherish, maybe?
His name, not cold, nor white, nor winter-born,
Just one syllable, like that whiteness,
Turned shorter to catch attention from its written length,
B&B their letters gave them, no overnight and morning serving,

Just two soundly pronounced full names,
Like their clarity of dislikes and their desire to display them,
Seemingly ready to punish that worshipped eldest,
Son of not theirs, nor brother of theirs, nor lover of theirs,
He left to live his life,
And live he did well, and loved he was longer by both mothers, than
    they were to be deemed

She was to descend, not of their mocked ways,
But all through her growing woman and wife's years,
That, not skin, nor lung, nor nervous, but boned fragility came down
    on her,
Seizing upon all bodily bends,
Such that even her head could not turn to him or away from them,
Till her passing took away all her need of glimpsing, or focusing on her
    knowing world's weakness

MY DECEITFUL BROTHER

(About my mother's brother – or who she thought was her brother –
actually only her cousin)

Not until then, not until now,
There's nothing so bad for a woman than a man who thinks he's good,
But what if he is good and knows it?
Everyone worshipped that eldest,
Charmingly good looking, he always enjoyed their throng,
Loved by all mothers and aunts,
All he knew was our kinship,
All he gave us was his greatness

Inside he was torn, boy he must have been,
To be able to be what he knew he always was,
Then he could not do that, even with his all-round celebrants,
As they and that would be lost, if he acted to be himself

So, swing with them he did,
Never edging that way,
Till he shocked them, one 50's day,
Leaving a letter, mothers read to them all,
And exiting the door without any more

How could they be,
Tears burned their hearts,
As wounds wept in their souls

My, how my mother's life was changed,
De, stroyed my faith in him, and them,
Ceit, how trusted love was lost,
Ful, never to be allowed to re-fill,
Bro, ken love, but not by his mother,
Ther, t'wer to be for me and for my son too

16

CHILD-MINDED

(About my mother's childhood with epilepsy and her brother's with asthma)

When alive, a child looks for innocence,
The younger you were, the less you received,
The older you were, the more you could look back at them and
    damage their naive selves

Two older than her, held her hand in that lingering image,
now held by me in my yearned for connection,
He the eldest, shone out all their love for him,
And their care, as he coughed and barely breathed,
They all knew he suffered, cautiously alive,
Yet they celebrated his strength to stand upright in his uncertainty,
She, never coughed, yet barely knew her uprightness,
Too fearful of shaking, falling, scaring their souls and driving their ease
    to mock,
Years upon years, she tried to cherish a little,
Too few days awake, no school, no nib, no written words, not now,
    not ever

How those silent times must have given you some peace,
Those noisy, shouty, senseless kids just wanted to show you what they
    thought of you,
How can two ill siblings get such different looks from others,
Fear just loves frowning on one, but fears focussed on both,
Saved only by your mother's warmth, no judgement by her, now or ever

How did that deceit aimed at her come about?
Centuries ago, it was determined by man that Illness was a weakness
    and that ongoing incurable medical problems were even worse,
At this time man pointed a discriminating finger at all those who were
    not "normal",

Man's inherent desire to show his hate of these was just that - inbuilt,
    part of humanity,
Children just followed this adult adultery,
Hence, those who suffered worst had to suffer even more,
The human genes inability to show love to those who need it most led
    to her childhood pain,
And left a legacy that fired at others,
Difference is not evil...

YOU'RE A QUEER ONE SHEILA BALDWIN

(Coming out to my mother: both my mother's brother/cousin and me)

Full of love yet
Never do we know from your words, what you feel
Brenda didn't
Doris didn't
Audrey didn't

What did you think of him?
What did you want him to think of you?
You're a queer one, what does that mean?
What did it mean to you then and what might it mean to you now?

Never did you really express your feelings,
What were you hiding, what were you scared of?
But your touch and the look in your eyes revealed all,
Calling us, caressing us, filling us, touching us all with your unspoken
    love

Queer to you and all of us,
Your soul diverted your inner reach from your outer reach's certainty
    of never revealing,
Until one day he left and another day I decided I might be left,
"Leave"; we did not expect the word to have a deeper meaning,
Just moving elsewhere, we were,
Knowing our inner and outer truths' human image,
And also, the desire to reach other worlds, not stay only in one,
Then according to your façade's face, we had transgressed somehow,
    in what way we both knew not,
Him, sixty-five years ago, me just forty,
A hundred years of our queer agony

VIEWING THE BLITZ

Imagined sirens fill the sky,
As they three, walk up the quiet country lanes,
To that Fosse Way crossing of the Long Itchington road,
Perched high above the Warwickshire downs,
With its valley view down to the Coventry city heights

Well, wartime young children they were, but this was no crashing plane,
Nor the release of an un-used bomb,
Nor the rush of the little girl and boys to their play place, air raid
    shelter, built swiftly by their Grumpy Gramp Dad, into their garden
    slope,
The sky that day was ablaze with a panoply of golden hues,
All day, they stared aghast, fuelled with fear,
Families, friends, streets and homes were up in flames,
Sky-filled terrors of newly arrived lines of gruesome planes and their
    searching hounds,
Passing by their returning devil fellows,
Minute after minute, hour after hour, day and night, till the dawn's
    awful reality shone the new sun on that torn town

These children, my mother, her sister and brother,
All mesmerised, in traumatised memory of that night,
Fixed as it was to become too in me,
through her routinely flared eyes as she glanced 'cross to that same
    skyline,
as we traversed that said crossroad on our journeys to her mother, my
    wartime grandmother

A STITCH IN TIME SAVES NINE

Dorothy was her closest friend,
They worked up town threading their days,
Chatting as dresses and numbers were tumbled away on the right,
On the left, thoughts of their togetherness, reached beyond the newly
   made hems of their skirts,
Dances, dinners, dates and daughters

Onward they must have gone, sorting colours, textures and styles,
Not rushing, but relishing their preparations,
Dresses to impress whichever soldiers came their way,
Which town hall or village dance hall, I remember not,
But seated in eager patience, together they glimpsed his walk through
   that place's door,
Then t'wards each other they turned,
A smile broader than a ship's beam,
Her man, they hoped, but knew, had come

Twenty years on, she still sits, knitting those glorious warming gifts,
One for him, two for us, twined with her united colours,
We relish those tours of the circular market,
Crowded, we hang on, as she picks one cloth and then another, for all
   her dresses self-made in our world,
And now twenty more years beyond,
Me and mine cherish most, a dig and a dash through that fixed
   shelves' beloved treasures,
Woollen meshes, entwined by her masterly hands,
Her beautiful stitches in time, stretch out to be my link to her life,
   saved nine times, but still not enough to live longest

PART II

NO BATMAN DOWN SOUTH, ONLY A ROBIN WATCHING AND FOLLOWING YOUR FORK

(About my father deciding whether to leave the Royal Marines or stay for seven more years working in South Africa as a batman)

Thirteen years a-rolling,
Over the ocean's waves,
Then that sergeant doctor,
Called you to his room,
"I offer you seven years more,"
"Come with me to be my batman,"
"Cape Town would be your home,"
"Could you two make this choice?"

Imagine my world, had that happened,
Childhood: twins in tow of their marine boy,
Criss-crossed seasons, same time zone,
Over-heated in all respects,
Spectacle of mountain coastal landscape,
Along the two southern oceans,
Apart-tight, surging unlawful life,
We would have had to live and observe those rising tides

Seven years down there we would have been,
Our universe and inside selves changed,
None of my self, all of what I know now,
Save the inner body soundly fixed,
But no gentle Warwickshire airs,
No carousel of aunts, no neighbourly cousins,
Or synchronised steps with the surrounding souls of my forebears

How did that sailor soldier on and make that call?
Fears inside of how to risk ourselves, but only then just two,
She could not leave home and family,
How could her illness be safe outside?
Too much doubt, too much uncertainty,
Too much to be unveiled, perhaps,
Stay he must,
Leave that man to another,
Walk through the marine's exit door,
Resting his head, daily, he knew not where,
He must have umm'd and ahh'd so long,
Then a nod or was it a shake,
And he knew what would never be their life's mistake

Rapture must have led to a new passion in their embrace,
As doubling their entwining, drew us two into them,
Together, surrounded by familiar ones we all would be,
That garden and its attraction gave us that new nature,
As our resigned batman, embraced his new robin, as it watched and
    followed that oft used digging fork

SOUTHSEA, OUR FIRST HOME WAITING FOR YOU TO COME

(Where my parents lived, before my father left the military in 1960, the year we were born)

Dancing on rollers, looking like ice skates,
But twins, same dressed, white on blue, we were on that ice,
Innocent glances at the sun's shadows, in the middle of that glistening
   lake,
Two days stay, whilst they rekindled our birth,
And us two, seeing His sea, being their blessed boys,
Meeting, we did, our only time, their motherly years old landlady,
That one, who filled Her days, as He rolled and swayed over the oceans,
She would go to that "aunts" phone to take a call on His ships' re-arrival,
Before counting the hours.....

As we dreamt of the glimmering ice rink made of concrete,
Which shined, as we danced away our unknown memories, of our
   soon to be conception

WHEN THE CHILDREN ARE ASLEEP, THEY'LL DREAM OF US

(In the voice of my parents)

Rocking them gently, beside our bodies,
Twin entwined with twin,
Hour after nightly hour,
We joined them to ourselves,
All akin next to our soft skin

As we drifted off, our minds managed our mood,
Thinking of being inside their heads,
Watching their flickering child's souls,
Deeply dreaming of their dreams,
Knowing or needing to see us on the screens of their visions,
We sighed, as we smiled, seeing our loving eyes, as the focus of their
    deep contentment,
Their double breaths, seeped into our heart filled lungs, in the home
    that was our Warwickshire womb

MY GIRL HILARY

(Would my mother's child be a girl or a boy – Hilary was to have been my name. In the voice of my mother)

He says to me, smiling with joyful mirth,
We are going to be giving birth,
So, now, I am getting to fill fast with your growing worth,
All I want is to hear your inner touch,
As I fear my self-doubts, oh so much

Here you are, I feel your presence soundly,
You will be my daughter, that I have sought so madly,
Teasing and pleasing, we will jump and shout together proudly,
I will gather needles and cotton and cloth, to make my clothes to
    show your beauty,
The vanguard of my existence is what you will shine out in so purely

But, hey, let me pause, what, what, what if it's a boy?
My head is spinning,
but unlike your swirling self,
I can't just swim to release my cries,
No, I cannot swim, I cannot swim,
and even if I could, I have no mother's water, in which to keep my
    troubled mind immersed

That boy, what would he be?
Upright, strong, certain, he will be my inner failing's, turned, fervent,
    fortitude,
Shining lightly, yet deeply into the world,
Like that other man, who shone out from his small farming, yet great
    sailing's outer worldly connection,
Little, honest, partner seeking me, who he gladly found,
Like him, you will be my right hand of goodness

Just think, the best boy can also be the best girl too,
Give him my cherished wishes, and those of my mothers, and he'll
    surely relish,
A little of my girl Hilary will trickle in that boy,
But no, surely not, no way,
not if there will be two,
No twins will come this way

TWO BOYS: TWO ARMS AROUND,
TWO CHAIRS TO REST, TWO LEADS TO HOLD

Here I am, me her first born and last born,
Leaving her far too long ago - 26 lost years,
Now our 40 years, like their 40 years soon to be surpassed,
But looking back, never looking forward, only days and sometime a
    few weeks allow me to stay certain

Here now, backward I ponder, and reflect on her,

We came, unplanned, unknown, mid-wife apart, thirty days before,
One, me, yanked he be, came out first, pain to see, her, no - him, no
    name now to know him by,
Then aided least, twinned he needed to be, swam quickly through her
    body to join him too, two it now be, together again they were

Clothed and worshipped by mountains of aunts,
One arm around each,
Vicar mirrored that holding and blessing us one year on,
Singing later was to come,
For now, our world was with her:
Double-prammed,
Then double pushed,
Whilst in town, no dog to take on lead,
Just two boys, equally pushy,
When walking aside her shopping,
Shoulders bound by un-keyed leads, to stop any shoves, this way or that

Most abiding dreams are of that triangular walk to Warwick,
Him off the chair showing us, he dashed,
Then him, back to sleep and me off to search for cows, or sheep, or
    soon to be gone elm tree clouds,
And then, images of bustle in a bus, firmly holding her coat, from behind,

We stop, leads connected and on with the leash, to Liptons,
Ladies around, looking, smiling, gossiping,
Watching us two, searching for tea or toast,
Never further than two feet from her hands, nor four from each of
our thumping hearts,
Too much lust for life and it's love for learning,
To keep our bodies engines tuned, and tended, well enough, for the
long lives we hoped we deserved

ALL IN A ROW TO BENDY BOW

Catch the pigeon or kill the crow

Wandering the lanes those long hot summer days,
Sweaty ladies adjacent to us two, dry, six-year-old boys,
Rounding the bends of the river Itchen,
The open fields attract their childhood nostalgia,
And we grab our hands all in a row

Swinging and swaying across the whole lane,
We sing that ancestral country song,
Ready to throw the one held firmly on the right,
With a tossing thrust, all of the way to bendy bow,
Across, in front of the other four, to the other side,
And then, the tune is on again, for the next pigeon or crow, to be
    thrown to their end

THAT WINDING ROAD TO HER HOME

I remember sitting astride, behind my mother,
My brother astride, behind my father,
On their old rusty bicycles,
Leaving for the hour, or was it two,
Up and down, round and round,
Journey in the summer warmth,
Down those small, town roads to village lanes,
Via the gentle, but not slight, crossings of those Warwickshire hills
    and valleys,
To her mother's home

As we swung, our heads balanced, to catch the glimpses,
Of those rural scenes, that defined the outlook, for all those forebears
    that came before,
First was the little town, on the edge of our town,
Strange name, what did it mean?
And how should we say that second word?
Again and again, we laughed varying its sound with another sound -
    Radford Semele,
But blink in those jokey moments and that junction had gone

Onward and upward, but not afore the scary and wary crossing of the
    big canal,
Grand Union of what?
Who knew, save the thrill of our smiles, as we rode it's bridge down at
    Radford's Bottom,
Parents inhale deeper more, as we rise to the crossing of the Roman way,
and it's view north to that great destroyed city of Coventry,
Then, gather and tense, as we approach the route's one big choice,
That blackberry-coated four-gated lane?
or the great descent with its treacherous turn on Snowford Hill?
The hill won on the way there, back home we would run and open the
    gates on that fruited lane, one by one

Once down the hill, we could breathe the adrenaline away,
and then glide the last mile of calm straights, to the turn to that street,
and its house and her unfathomably always warm welcome, to us two,
The relentlessly rugged and tough twosome kids that we were,
She relished our presence all her life

THOSE CURLERS OF DECEPTION

Ten metal rods, symmetrically aligned,
Piercing through the toy's battery base,
Plugged in, to fire their sword-like thrusts,
Contained, when cold, in a crusty oblong plastic top,
Taken to my small, four by four room, to test its strength

When hot, those hair hunters would be inserted onto the steel,
Then, one by one, those curlers would be coiled up close to her skull,
amidst the long damp rugged locks of her precious hair,
Letting them rest in their locking and setting lotion,
She would delicately remove them, to leave a gently releasing motion,
Of soft, outward and inward smiling locks, of her dark blond hair

So, then she would stand unlike before,
Richly displayed, with hair-scented spray,
Marching or just moseying down the alleys of her life,
Confidence, constructed abreast her life's common downward existence,
But now, standing high, aside her new man and boys,
She shone, with those curing curlers,
Deceiving all .... or none?

SOAPING TO STOP ITS SEEPING

What does a child fear most?
How does their body connect to their youthful mind?
Parents give you that certainty over fear,
Direct you, lead you, bring solace,

I can go round and round trying to shed light,
But there is no reality, nothing I know, will ever be right,
Then, unlike now, when all seems certain,
All you had, was the fragility of being just a little person

What brought you, tiny you, full of their security,
To suddenly shudder in physical insecurity,
Pock-marked finger that would bring me that un-named disease's
    walk of shame,
Tummy felt lump, that would tip me, night after night, into that too
    well named, killer shadow's blame,
Those two sure, as all was sure, fallacies, convinced me of knowing my
    bodies pain

So mother, you were, ready you were,
To do all things you knew to do,
A woman's touch,
Clearing up from even our own touch

Glimpsing into the radiant clouds,
That hide my momentarily caught past thoughts,
I wonder, how I came to be me,
These nightmare lightning bolts, just told,
And their precursors,
Made me know I would gain something, somewhere, somehow, to be
    like thee
Those touches from her must have taught me naught, as the physical,
    emotional, existential and the essential, would not let me not be me

36

MARAZION CLEANER

(The student accommodation called Marazion House where my mother cleaned)

Here we are driving to the end of our kingdom,
As we pass by the furthest Cornish capital Penzance,
We look out the window and see a signpost,
As I notice that word, next to St Michael's Mount,
My passenger map reading role disappears, in a mirage of being
    thrown back to my childhood

Her seamstress life was over,
As we held her up and took over her days,
School took us away and her fingers itched for a few pennies and
    useful hours,
Cleaning those two friend's homes helped,
But not enough, and she joined the student's days herself,
Relishing and rummaging their youthfulness,
She took over their own mother's role in their university hostel hotel
    called Marazion House

And now, that full-rounded word, repeated by me, so many times,
Reminds me of that Victorian home, those student's first homes away
    from their own homes,
Down the street from my boy's college,
Where I would stroll, some lunchtimes,
To watch the view from that saint's mount,
As the tide unconnected, then connected me to them,
As she tidied their rooms and made their beds,
Like their mothers would do back home,

It made me, and her, much less tongue-tied over my future departure,
seven years down to one year, from them,
There will always be a place name here to keep us closer to wherever
far away we are,
And Marazion, filled me with that verbal, ink-nibbed touch of distant
places, and their descent to me and my world

HERALD STUCK ON PORLOCK, SHEILA STUCK IN NEUTRAL

A laugh wasn't quite the word to have expressed what we felt,
A giraffe wasn't quite tall enough to have seen over the hill,
Drafts wouldn't be quite the game to tell this risky tale,
A calf wasn't how we felt, children though we were

As our navy-blue four-pointed triumphant family car,
Rolled us, four am, pre-dawn dark, from our mid-country home,
Along the roller-coaster Roman road,
Through adjoining counties, to the moor tops of Devon,
North we would go, tars and steps, blooming heathers and gorse,
Till we descended to those great flooded upper and lower villages of
    Lynton and Lynmouth,
Afore we twisted the valleys last curve and glimpse of the cliffs to
    the sea

That acute, slow, final turn was to be that Herald's last, we thought,
Mother, new driver, who learnt that skill, when he was locked up in a
    hospital bed,
Women drive only when men are sick?
After the bend, so un-revealed afore, the road went steep, yea so
    steep,
But assured as she was by then, her yearned for learning a-driving,
Never told her how to keep a-forward,
Which gears, which foot, which hand, and oh! what! another car
    ahead,
Too much to keep her and our momentum, and the Herald stalled,
Backward, downward, we started creeping, till that man lurched his
    hands and pulled on that hand's brake and ... phew we breathed
    and sighed in stationary relief,
Till she tried and tried again, and again, to start without stalling,

Then the drafts and the laughs began by these young calves,
It became a chance game, till our relentless laughing told her it's end
   game,
Get out and let him take on that vertical challenge,
So, he did, and military man that he was, he jerked us up, third time
   of asking, onward and up to the next moor top

TWISTING THE MINCER, MINCING THE TWISTER, EATING THE REMNANTS

Playing with her machines,
Helping her stressful cooking,
Fearful of the working blades,
Fingers or elbows or chins,
All might disappear,
Never leaving anything to be thrown away,
All were thrown into my mouth

SWIRLING ON THE POOF

It sits there still,
Three legs firmly to the ground,
Old red leather, bounding its half soft seat,
Each short, vulnerable, leg, upholds its duty to the other two,
Grandmother's chair's place, always on my carpet, by each home's
    front window,
Not that this little poof could see outside

So now, I slump down on the low doughy seat,
And close my eyes to recollect those childhood times

As Gran would charge us with tasks and games,
We sat put, one at a time,
in our attempts to get free from her reach,
We would kick our tiny feet hard on the thick carpet,
First pushing right, letting us spin clockwise,
Spiralling till our hair pointed to the stars,
Each would connect, then free us for
the other foot to shove us the other way round,
Rubbing the edges of our shorts against our too delicate thigh's skin,
We often yelped in a little pain, but freely we were happy,
On the poof's level swirling freedom plain

TOM AND JERRY, THE CHICKENS WERE LAST

One April, when we were less than ten,
We drove in that green rounded mini, six cramped within,
Up to their best, known farmers yard,
Those smells were so new to us boys,
Fragrant sewage and worse we thought,
But hands in hands, Mum and Gran, walked us to their back

Easter gifts were to be bought for us gemini two,
We thought naught as they chatted and reminisced,
Then back to the car we stepped, circular cardboard box carried,
    no bigger that our feet,
Then slowly we rushed as we drove back to my Gran's Southam
    Road home

That garden with its uphill slope,
Wartime brought a shelter under its rise,
from the bombers who failed to drop on their closest city,
So young she was, how painful that must have been,
Back yard with mangle and that deep copper pot,
And a corner that was to house their gift

Aunt's budgie cage, long gone bird, but that was to be their home,
Twenty-one tiny yellow chicks were ours,
Our surprise and joy, was so full,
As we tickled and rubbed their fluffy tiny selves,
They were fed by some and stayed for just a week,
When as sudden as we arrived, all bar six, were returned to their
    farm,
Or that's at least what we were told,

Those six we nurtured and told,
Kind little tales as they grew and turned from yellow to white,
Five months of jumping around, up and down that long garden,
Then grandpa says, they will taste good,
So, one by one, his role was to end each,
Then plucking and preparing we stunned ourselves by eating them all,
But the last two were saved for longer by our befriending and
    children's love of Tom and Jerry,
That cartoon, of cat and mouse, or chicken twins?
Filled us with smiles and desire never to lose,
But old man Arch would not hear no,
And two weeks later Tom first, then afterwards Jerry,
We learned that nothing was for ever, least of all them, or us

LYING IN BED BESIDE LIVE FLESH

Looking back in time, to those day after days,
From their unconscious start to their conscious end

In the morning world of their bed,
Remembering always having been there, or just gently
opening the door, lifting the light sheets, and
sliding into the dark warm space between live flesh

Why am I using that word..... flesh?
It sounds like water, as it rushes over rocks, as I say it out again,
And that's the feeling that the touch of soft smooth skin, on a body
    gave me

Who's live flesh?
The cellular mirror of myself?
The emotional echo of her son?
The genetic parallel of my own live flesh?

This flesh on flesh, gave sought after nourishment,
and fed me with sensual desires,
Unconscious, delicious, precious,
Locking in a life enriched with need and sure of its form and feeling,
This never-ending need and fear of its loss,
Made optimism internal, surrounded by a thick skin of pessimism

So, what about the touch?
My feet and toes slide glistening down the body
and sparingly hairy legs of my deliverer,
Belly on belly, magical rubbing tells my body its source,
Arms and hands reach out for the neck......
The place that woke massage senses,
Fingers and palms pressing hard on tender muscles,
Lips close in on red skin, as blood rushes to kiss them,

Pre-pubescent sexual awakening in the arms of a mother,
I must not have been naked but only remember being so,
Layers rolled away by deep memory waves,
Warmed and secure, I roll my body over,
The gap I fill edges me closer to another...

What is this hair, itching my softness?
Bones and muscles, no mother has,
My reminisced nudity fuels great fear,
Unspoken and almost unconsciously I recollect,
Recoiling, hoping not to see a father's child organ,
Shrivelled in its jealous search for
a mother's warmth given to her new flesh
I begin to shiver and shudder and have to turn back

Daylight was not there, but slowly the curtains begin to lighten,
Bang!!
goes the door and in jumps my other half
No tender caresses sought by this one,
Just a desperate need for warmth and day duties to avoid,
He squeezes between the bed's edge and the child organ carrier and
    goes still.....
Sensing something more, something I carried,
He slimily slides over father's chest and tries to push me out,
The one was two,
But two now had to become one
And demanding all I had, he replaces me..........

CHANGING BEDROOMS

My first conscious defining moment as me,
Choosing to be on my own,
Leaving my womb brother's dream room,
Here's how it came to be

I have no memory of my place in David's room,
Just a hidden certainty of its truth,
Like all those things from long before,
That you only heard about from others,
And which now became your past,
But this recall is truly mine
            firmly in its original space

Mother came so urgent to inquire,
Nothing neutral in her look,
One question, so keenly searching for an answer,
"Do I want a place just for me?"
How could I understand its meaning,
Me versus me and him, what did that imply?
To sit, rest, sleep, wake, work................alone
Solitary and separately,
My things just for me,
My decisions, my life from now on,
My own window, my own outlook,
How could a content, happy, lucky boy say no,
The day passed and my hope was filled with excitement
But it was soon
to be slammed with a brutal reality

Same mother, same look, came by again
quick to tell, as before, sure of her mind
"if you leave David's room"
(already defined, no longer mine)

"we will never let you go back!"……
CRASH……………
The walls have fallen, the floor collapsed,
Falling to sit astride my new existence,
Me, not me and him,
It was our shared womb, but only my placenta,

Only can I rely on me, from now on
15 years of liberating solitude followed,
Until my choices led to my second David,
And then 15 years later, when she had departed,
Father returned me to my brother's room,
For 20 more years of re-feeling

Now he has gone, the room is gone,
No bedrooms to move to or back from,
I can reflect …….
Eventual gratitude for her helping me to take that first step alone…

HANDKERCHIEFS ON THE BOIL

Imagined lurgies longing to live,
Pollen passing from plants to the air,
Blown long and hard into the skies of our home,
Casually descending as the breeze eases,
Hovering at human height

Naive twins tussle with teenage torments,
Laugh and cry, run and fly, breathe and lie,
Innocent inhalations,
Taking the tiny flora dust into themselves,
For days and nights of sticky eyes, blocked and runny noses,
Sneezed or blown or tear dropped,
Onto the white soft cloth of their mother's making, embroidered with
  their names

To be repeated, day after early summer day,
until June ends its sky-filled grass and tree offspring days,
Each dawn piles of yellow, sticky, possibly infected, handkerchiefs
  need cleansing,
Thrown into mother's selected steel pot,
They must be liquid roasted and rid of their dirty richness,
Pegged on the garden's nearest line to keep their blemishes hidden,
Dried in the heat and rushed to the hankies' draw in the nearest
  cupboard,
Low enough to be grabbed open by us
and seized as the next days 'bless-you' seeking sneezes begin again,
22 for him and 19 for me,
Or so the records say..

LETTUCE UP THE SKIRT

How can a lettuce laugh last so long?

Limp and flat, once picked, they all become,
If not, they ravish the sunshine and reach for the sky,
shooting upward to try to flower ...to nothing,
And leaving those left salad leaves to a shrivelling, wasteful end

Those days of youth when all you knew of these leaves was their
    tastelessness,
No relish, no flourish, no rush to reach the plate,
On which they rested, dry and untouched,
Save the dripping colours of the so-called delight of their coloured
    friends,
Chastened flavours of red and green,
And the tainting drips of that purple root's fruit

Were my memories of those times to cherish?
There were none for me but one,
Abreast my searching soul, as I rode the waves this way and that,
    north and south,
I sat, a weekend back home, beside my quiet father and buoyant
    brother,
Lounging as we waited, slow arm-chaired watching the windowed
    sunset,
As a murmuring began somewhere,
Who or what, we all three glimpsed knowing not,
And then a louder sound came, a shout or something else,
Followed by another,
I dashed to the door and then to the other door,
Astounded I must have sounded, when I threw myself into that
    kitchen

Mother smothered by a spitting fit, no breaths possible,
As she gasped her massive smiles and lung filled laughs,
Thrusting her way towards her mother,
Who looked lost in her step, as she cried out relentless tears in her
    utter happiness,
Their eyes looked fixed in playful childhood menace as they battled
    for something,
Then I saw their game, one that I was not to join,
Scattered on the floor were bruised torn fragments of that green leaf,
And as I returned my glance to both of them,
The now revealed battle recommenced

Leaves in the sink were sunk in its cold water,
Once, a while ago, this would have been just for cleaning their soiled
    surfaces,
Each had to be grabbed by one of them, or both,
The cold, trickling, handfuls would be held low,
As the other hand stretched to grab the edge of their opponent's dress,
And throwing the dress out, the leaves were thrown up,
Followed by the next grunt of the attacker and the next scream of the
    attacked,
Which led to the longest squirming laugh a woman could make,
And then the next leaves were lifted and thrown, and the next,
Mother and grandmother clearly had played this childless children's
    game before,
Adding to its elongated momentary pleasure through their many
    memories,
Thus, making it the longest lettuce laugh I had ever heard

In that moment, I knew I would always love the memory of that day
and it's game,
It stays in my mind as the most joyful lament of their now departed
    souls

HIGH HEELS

Mid-teens, tense emotions, routine rebukes,
But I just knew, from the time's magical music and band's attire,
That a certain dress code was required if my worship of them was to be,
That meant trousers that flared beyond your feet,
And shoes, which took you inches higher to a platform you could
    never see

However, so juvenile we were, adults we dreamt of, but were not,
Morning over, the school bells rang and out we swung,
Racing to make the hunger linger no longer,
Hanging hands around the stairwell to jump down the steps to join
    the lunch queue,
But not me, not that time, not that day,
Those heels slipped and scurried me irregularly down the stairs into a
    heap,
Bent bones, platforms awry, ankle broken, or at least I thought

Agony that day, taken home, doctor's the next,
No broken foot, or any limb, but no high heels for a week,
Then my mind had to face up to its first, possibly futile, choice,
Lit by the medic's mention of my potential mutation,
Toes and feet facing too far out than normal ones should,
My ankles had grown with double-jointed jars,
Too much pressure had been pushing them past any certain
    uprightness,
So, fall I did and further down I could have been destined to diminish

Poor Martin machinated, and slept sorely for too many days,
Then knew he must just push his feet, inner up and outer part down,
Walking wobbly at first, solidly later, fusing his brain's barbaric brush
    with the doctor's danger,
Keeping the joint one way and never, even if jokingly, jutting the other,
But mother had another plan,

Maybe just to plant this teen,
with a fear of never raising himself up on those blissful heights of
    fashionable heels again,
and tarnished with joking jibes from all around be they friends and foes,
With her choice, iron-man he was not to be,
Iron clad, his legs would be,
Calibrated and calipered, nailed and sealed, they would never wrongly
    move,

One week on, and for years to come,
I never wore those high heels,
Shoes to glamour myself were naught,
My ankles and feet found their own strength to stay strong, no metal
    mounts,
Leaning not on the left but the feet's right
As nature meant them to be
That limb's arch was found by my fortitude
And the double ankle, as with my double-jointed thumb, and all my
    life's feared doubles,
Kept alone for my own introspection as I looked out from my imaginary
    high heeled platform
covered by my wide flared trousers listening to my old 70's soul
    music 45's.

THAT QUESTION

Lessons done, exams passed,
Years of relentless learning, converted into results,
Parents grateful, their only vivid feelings,
Summer to think ahead, new school, new friends

Letter from Williamson, Headmaster to family headmistress,
Mother asked to join me in meeting that man,
No father, no other, meeting for what purpose?
Dressed well, Mother would make sure I was

She nervous, me confused, off we went,
Grand town's grandest building
Wide street, wealthiest residents, tree's canopy shading them,
Bell rung, we wait outside, two chairs, not together

Called in, he shakes our hands and invites us to join him at his table,
The other side of it, of course,
Welcoming her, welcoming especially me,
Congratulating my success at getting there

Then those questions:
"Do you have any brothers or sisters?" he asks,
"One brother, David", she breathlessly, stubbornly says,
"David, my twin brother", I add automatically, stoically,
"Do you want me to get him here too?" he seemingly,
     casually replies
Minor pause, no reflection, just a short inhalation and then she
     almost cries out,
"No, no, that's OK, but no"

His question and her reply shocked, surprised and shunted me
    for ever,
I thought, but did not say,
"Why not bring him here too?"
"Why is he able to bring him here?"
"No rules that I felt were real were unchangeable, surely?"

NEVER MORE NO CLUES

Wendy, Janice and David,
The clues are in the names

As long as I knew,
All others were few,
But these five she relished,
Always to be cherished,
Deep in her soul was June,
Who sadly left her, so soon,
Sooner than she,
but following her, she soon t'would be

That short walk, up the road, to the right, then a short skip to her
    charmer,
Franklin, Moorhill, then we are there at Washbourne's corner,
In that house, that loving, living room, piano besides,
I would sit and feel mesmerised by their adult lives,
And in this place, and this one alone, I was allowed, encouraged,
    motivated to engage,
And ask one question after another, to learn more of all their minds'
    sage

Their piano was always my most missed link,
The closest I got to those notes, those rhythms, those auras,
David the youngest to learn its joy went from piano to organ,
They came to my city, to that place, with June, to envelop their joy at
    his new priestly role,
Wendy, we knew most, as closest she was to us by age and in my
    class,
She trifled with those white keys, but never so soundly sure was she
    to be as that boy that followed her
She did though join my chosen ten, and her chosen ten, to be with in
    our north town learned place,

So once or twice, we met along our adjoining road, and then only
    once in our staged dramas,
She married one of my school kids, not that it lasted long, no children,
Janice, oh that sweet middle one, big glasses, most like June,
No knowledge of her way down her path,
No clues to know how she lives or lived,
No connection to all,
Save the glimpses left or right, as we swiftly passed by their old corner
    house,
No more gathering evenings,
Nor shared meals or games or piano keys,
Never more no clues

OUR MAGICAL MUSIC BOX

It was placed with delicacy and reverence in my mother's room,
Seemingly floating on the surface of a shining dark oak cabinet,
It had an enticing scent that filled its air and kept you from leaving

It belonged to my mother's, mother's, mother.....
I knew not what age it had been born,
It always belonged there, as they did

In later life, I now rush to my audience seat,
To await the pleasures of a familiar named piece of music,
But if Grieg's nineteenth century Bergen life knew it or not,
The opening bars of his piano piece's slow movement unlocked the key,

How can just a few notes created to fill the ears with pleasure,
Shimmer the body with emotion and moisten my face with tears of joy,
Telling those keys to climb out of their vault,
Fly to the sacred cabinet and turn the lock of that magic box,
Thus, connecting the generations to each other

At first all I see with those few notes is the slow opening,
Of the dark emerald box lid with its golden embosses,
But who is gathering around to share that innocent rapture?
Loving, familiar women, resting their faces on the cabinet's lacquer,
    smiling together

Each touch of the piano keys, shines into glistening warmth,
As the lid opens revealing the red velvet cover,
Platform for two, but now only holding one,
A delicate ballerina turning slowly to that, at first slow, then rushing,
    ecstatic melody,
She turns and finds her partner missing,
Then again, she turns and smiling with joy towards all those around,
Her lonely sadness is transformed into her dance's blissful melancholy

The jewelled box is her world but its
Shimmering perfection protects and its
Music's delicate certainty envelopes her home
And gives me, the memory listener,
A joy that radiates indescribable power and emotion,
Taking me back to those days of my childhood,
When alone I would occasionally come to that quiet room and turn
that key

SHE SINGS HIS PRAISES

He tends her woefully grieved wounds
Their "love" is transcribed
In the mixed-up mixture of love,
usefulness and pride

An exclusive praise-service company

WE'LL NEVER WALK ALONE

(The day I had my graduation – after I had met my David – with my parents and grandmother)

Crowds walk towards,
Gathering from all places,
Surrounding all together,
Young honours exalted

Three you were with me,
No singing only praising,
But the gulps of tension,
Flattered the day's attention

Grandmother's loving aged eyes,
Mother's honoured swooning looks,
Father's presence's feelings sought,
My success's gratification known

Again, I felt the world's saluting halo,
Support, strength, all as one,
You, me, they, will sway to
where we choose, never to lose

Choirs, communities, friends, workplaces,
Runners, swimmers, pedallers, walkers,
Sounds, breaths, feelings, touches,
Time brings time, no time brings no time

PART III

RACING IN THAT HEAVY BLACK CAR

(My grandmother's funeral. I was told of her passing, not the day it happened but a day or two later after my first professional exams had finished – ironically I failed them)

Angled beside my sad mother's grief,
No certain love, like the resting lady, who we were following fast,
Round that too sloped curve beside the bluebell wood of our body's
    eternity

I heard the bell and had the call, not on the day my beloved Gran
    breathed her last,
But not till my supposedly yearned for profession's starting point had
    ironically failed,
Had I called in bereft, I might have second chanced my chance of
    getting where both mothers felt I
should securely be,
But gladly, my life worked that moment around,
But not hers, not my startled loss,
Not my stark reality of her shocked life curtailing loss,
Never no more, would her firm love's deliverer hold her,
And be there to keep her solid in her coming years of fragility

So, delivered from that upright shaking right hand slope, towards that
    resting place,
Out we went in leaning, stepping unison,
To follow her into that haloed chapel,
Never have tears so rushed down all our cheeks,
No recognition of those watered eye's connection to our souls,
Not this grief, that would only come to me half my life later,
Sadness was sadness, loss was loss, no recognition of old aged
    reflection on love,
and its deep touch of the memory's real presence of those now gone

LONDON CALLING

Yes, they would descend to my place,
That early 90's Christmas time,
My plentiful joy, stymied by missing him,
To Cambridge he would be

That turkey, that tree, that cake, that pudding,
I would need to collect and lay out,
Placing away my coming jubilation,
To focus on the tasks ahead

My home, them coming to celebrate with me,
Cannot remember where my brother was to be,
But little did I know this chance would be my only chance,
But nothing could have taken away my anticipated trance

Then to make it happen, I heard that I needed to drive,
To their, my Whitnash home, carrying them and their gifts, I had to
    rush, to strive,
No driving for them, no familiar train route, they just would not take,
So, loading up, next day, we set off back south, did they both seem to
    be not awake?

Two hours later, my Post Office house, showing them the park and its
    view,
And taking their stuff to their suitably sleepy downstairs room, then
    making them a brew,
Whilst that tree beckoned her back, to rekindle our childhood joy,
She took out an angel she had stitched with a dress and ironed on her
    barbie wings, this was not a boy

My mother's bedecked angel stayed at the top of the tree,
That year and all those following, when the tree was big enough to
    hold her and for all to see,

Those childhood, or who knows from when before, baubles glistened
    beneath the angel, amidst the tinsel,
All to be carefully wrapped and kept in their ancient boxes, for those
    following years to be next to the window sill

The next day, Boxing as we call it, we ventured into that big city,
Showing them many of its glorious charms, although to mother it was
    rather gritty,
Quiet though its heights were not that day,
On such a holiday, then, not many places to dine were open and my
    mind went into disarray

Where could I take them to, to eat, and to enjoy?
Soho, was my only thought, and one big loud gay brunch bar, a hope
    that in our togetherness this choice would not destroy,
In we went and down we sat, quite quiet, but not silent,
A drink, and lunch was served, relishing they seemed and upward my
    heart went,
But then she caught, in her eye, and to my eyes, a glimpse of
    something certainly adroit,
Straightened head and no more smiles, just blinks, they both had
    finally clocked this gay place, no more my life's choice, despite this
    lovely meal, could their unknown knowledge to me, be something
    I could exploit

Not that sombre it did seem, the remaining two days,
But reality, as it does.... must have come back to them and their ways,
Maybe just that this Christmas was coming to an end,
And we three knew, in some unconscious way, that some things just
    would never mend

I then packed that car again, leaving so many mementos, the love of
    which would never fade,
Closing the gate of that Cadogan house front, that winter morn, which
    was, I knew, to remain in the shade,
David could then return to our home, as I drove back over the Chiltern
    Hills,

66

Dropping them at 59, Franklin Road, close by our neighbour's fence,
   all childhood thoughts, these words will always fill

Neither mother nor father would ever venture south to be with me,
Thirty years, filled with longing, and grief, it would be,
Sheila, merely a few Christmases more she would have left,
Harold, almost all those years alone he would be, cheerful but always
   he would be bereft

A SECOND STITCH IN TIME MIGHT SAVE NINE MORE PAINS

(About my mother's -and later my father's friend Ann)

School days took them both twice a day,
To walk with us and them, up the roads, to that gate,
That's when they met, but friends they did not, then, quite become,
Not till I had left that town to search for my life,
That was when, for whatever reason, they both re-joined themselves,
In a stitching club, one or some evenings, they met with twelve
    others,
Changing location from one to each other's homes,
Well befriended they did so become

Through her last fifteen years, they knitted and stitched to think and
    dress themselves,
And their husbands and now and again, their, not so little ones,
My last one was a bookmark, cross-stitched in memory of their
    fortieth year,
Now, as I read each book, it is entwined in every page, in which I rest
    for breath

But this special friendship with Ann gave more, much more,
She knew Mum fought internal battles, unshared, unresolved,
And on talking 'bout those childhood times, to Ann all became clear,
She too shared the same tough times but had sought not fought, and
    was now well at ease,
But once their kindred themes had been aired,
Ann felt a start to that journey she knew not just how long t'would be,
Stitching she thought it would simply be, with these two "old hands",
But although they entwined their threads on and on,
No clarity on the final shape, in sight, would come,
Not what she wanted me to be, stuck more on who I was,

Ann tried and tried and was loyal to the end,
When, then, she became my father's grieving listener and bringer
  back to look up at the world,
And then, when he left, to me, she came, and I came, and loyal
  reminder of their times and thoughts and affection she became

LYING BESIDE IN THE CARDIOLOGY WARD

I rested, as her heart rusted, struggling to understand or match its lust
    to thud at the speed of light,
Surrounded by bright lights and other worldly science, she struggled
    to comprehend,
Save when I kissed her and sighed in sadness, and lifted my legs up to
    lie beside her on that narrow well pillowed bed,
No glimpses, at that time, or anything other than her soothing joy and
    the reassuring adjacency of our head-to-toes being together

Two swift weekend drives up from home to my childhood home,
To go visit and lie beside her on that bed,
Then fortune came to her and the speed-of-light-beats changed back
    to more resting pulses,
And out she came,
For a few more years, head protected by that yellow bonnet,
Till her un-thrown dice dealt yet more tossed tumultuous times,
No more lying besides,
No more feeling her touch,
No more looks of love

THAT MOMENT WHEN THE PHONE CALL
CAME - COLLAPSING ME

Crazily rushing this way and that,
In my workplace, just above the circular entrance down below London
    Bridge,
Where on silly Saturdays, when I sometimes worked a morning,
I would happen upon an un-fearing, lazy fox, sleeping soundly in our
    revolving door,
Challenging me to see how I could enter

Those eight or ten working mates, beside the library and elevator,
    cheered our days,
But not this day,
Leaning against my chair, having glanced at the loud, other blonde
    leader, the other end of the group,
I heard the twenty-seventh call tone,
And reached for the phone, in my usual routine manner

My brother, hesitant and wobbly was his voice,
Slowly begun to tell me what he had to tell me,
And I slumped, heavier than ever, on my familiar chair,
Podding peas, she was, his garden's produce, her job to get them
    ready to freeze,
'Cept she was now frozen, heart reaching its speed of light, turned
    hers off,
She managed with her floppy breath and wobbling teeth,
To look at him and say goodbye

I looked about as my eyes were swimming in tears,
They all came and embraced my shoulders,
Looking lost, as I continued to feel my decline, taking me down into
    the earth,
That day, that second, I really started to fear

THEY TAUGHT ME LOVE

I am so lucky
And so grateful for their gift.

5 December 2018,
"Where is my watch?" "What is the time?"
"Here take mine Dad".

Placed firmly but gently around his delicate wrist,
My watch became his watch,
Our shared time stood still,
For a precious while.

But then the seconds began walking again,
And mine and his time inched invisibly forward,
Moving towards our last goodbye.

Now that watch joins my wrist again,
As I hold my arm out to rest his arms in the
arms of my mother.

Sending my life's gratitude for your loving gift,
As you depart.

For ever,
With Sheila and God,
And your love.

MOTHER, WHERE ARE YOU!!!

Between her legs I came

Between my legs I sit

Bewildered and lost

I AM SEARCHING FOR YOU MOTHER

I am searching for you mother,
Please hear me, my father is looking for you,
He wants to join you soon,
So, he needs your presence now

I have been searching for you since you left,
Or maybe since you left my love behind,
Nearly forty years of absence,
The pain has flooded and retreated
and flooded again,
My fears of your discarded love
have given me many traumas
Sometimes when the painful storms came,
Sometimes during the dry season,
But those daytime nightmares,
have fuelled my pessimism

Why my love for your love could be allowed, by you, to seep away
into the drains of your street,
Just because of my chosen love,
I will never know

But if you tell us where you are,
We can rekindle our touch together,
Those original gentle caresses,
From the affectionate feathers of my mother hen
and your gift to me.
Returned to you by my fluffy body,
muzzling against your soul

Let us back in – we cry
Let us in

WHY A MOTHER CANNOT LET GO

When swirling in her love,
She never knew what that would bring,
Staying home, not sailing south
Her ease then brought her soul to sing

Imagine those notes, simple yet charged,
They all heard them, those twelve and four,
Hailing someone, somewhere, to bring her more,
And so, those little fish did swim and find her door

She knew, he knew, we knew, as we together could feel,
Two very little swimmers deep inside her grew and grew
Till fears sent her awry, and well within she knew those two would
     win and be,
Of course, unconscious though it was, we all three knew it was not to
     be two but three

No one knew till one autumn night we started to fight,
And struggling to be free, me first them him, swished out into sight,
Existing within, being born from inside, how could we be aught but
     part of her,
And never before or then or beyond could either of us believe that it
     wasn't to be

How can I have lived in my world, however it was,
Believing our hands would always be held because...
Being not singular but only being part, making a whole only
     together,
That was nothing alone that was ever anything it was possible to
     fully treasure

Never let go, never part,
Never rip up, never let that start,
Always enveloped, always in love,
Always entwined, always our hands, will be, in one golden glove

THAT SUN BONNET

Resting unmoved for twenty-five years,
Waiting for the right opening of the adjacent door,
It gives me a glimpse and a sigh and a waft of her hair, every time I
   come and go by

She wore it, later in her life,
To fend off the sun's heart targeted rays,
It fitted my head, but, although my father had held it out,
I never placed it there, save once, to feel her head's circular uneven
    resonance

It accompanied her and me on our too few walks,
Most in my mind, down memory lane,
Is that photo of us wandering back, from Charlecote Park
deer all around, just does and fawns, no stags to challenge our
    together steps,
The park's delicious name, is it charlecote or chocolate? was relished
    also by our unsought forebear,
Who's written words still charm the world,
His mothers and their sons, twisted in sonnets,
Never heard by mine, just once by me,
But mingled in my deep thoughts this late spring morn

I long look at that golden straw bonnet,
Shimmering as its surface does when the sun comes near,
Delicately bound by her flower-patterned pale-yellow ribbon,
Showing those who passed by, and who cared to look, her weakened,
    but much relished seamstress's eye

Soon, we will not be near that familiar door,
Stretching and stressing, taking all that we have, to our final home,
    we hope,
My mother's millinery headpiece will accompany me,
Carried carefully by my ageing hands,
I will then feel and hear its natural sense,
And find its penultimate resting door,
There it will wait and watch my eyes,
As she waits short or not so short, or long or not so long,
For my final hours,

Knowing, as I know, that that matted straw and tied silk, and its
    weaver's touch,
Will join my skin and bones, in that wooden darkness,
Before ascending to her side, where we will share time, donning its
    shading cover,
In our bright, timeless embrace

ONE HAND, ONE HEART

Make of our hands, one hand,
Make of our hearts, one heart,
Make of our vows, one last vow:
Only death will part us now.

MARIA
Make of our lives, one life
Day after day, one life

BOTH
Now it begins,
now we start,
One hand, one heart,
Even death won't part us now.

Make of our lives, one life,
Day after day, one life
Now it begins, now we start
One hand, one heart
Even death won't part us now.

(Influenced by and most of the words taken from the song One Hand,
One Heart, from West Side Story, the song is by Ansel Elgort and
Rachel Zegler)

Four country barley folks, always flourishing together in and above the wheat fields, however, wherever, whatever we were to become....